·ARIANE DEWEY·

·PECOS· ·BILL·

GREENWILLOW BOOKS, NEW YORK

Library of Congress Cataloging in Publication Data

Dewey, Ariane.   Pecos Bill.
Summary: An account of the remarkable
exploits of legendary hero Pecos Bill.
1. Pecos Bill (Legendary character)–Juvenile
literature.   1. Pecos Bill (Legendary character)
2. Folklore–United States.   3. Tall tales] I. Title.
PZ8.1.D54Pe 1983   398.2′1′0973 [E]   82-9229
ISBN 0-688-01410-0   AACR2
ISBN 0-688-01412-7 (lib. bdg.)

FOR AVA AND LIBBY

Pecos Bill was born in Texas
a long time ago.
His family lived
hundreds of miles from anyone.

One day, some settlers
built a cabin fifty miles away.
"Let's move," Bill's mother said.
"It's getting crowded around here."

His parents packed their wagon
and headed west.
As they crossed the Pecos River,
the wagon hit a rock.
It tilted over and Bill fell out.

The current was swift
and carried him away.
His parents couldn't find him.
He would have drowned,
but an old coyote saw him
and pulled him
out of the water.

Bill stayed with the coyotes.

They raised him like a pup.

He learned to run with the pack.

He could howl at the moon.

He could do anything.

One day a cowboy came along.

"Hey, kid," he said,

"where are your clothes?"

"I'm not a kid, I'm a coyote,"
 Bill replied.

"I never saw a coyote without a tail,"
 said the cowboy.

Bill was upset.

"If I'm not a coyote, what am I?"
he asked.

"A boy and a big one at that,"
said the cowboy.

"Come with me and see for yourself.
But I'd better lend you some clothes."

He helped Bill put the clothes on.

"My name is Curly Joe.

What's yours?" said the cowboy.

"Bill," said Bill.

They were standing by the river.

"Pecos Bill sounds better,"

said the cowboy.

And that's how Pecos Bill

got his name.

The cowboy rode his horse
and Bill ran along beside him.
Suddenly a twelve-foot rattlesnake
struck out from behind a rock.
It sank its fangs into Bill's leg.

Bill grabbed hold of the rattler.

The snake fought hard,

but Bill fought harder.

He squeezed all the poison

out of the snake.

"I'm beat," the rattler finally hissed.

Bill coiled the snake up

and put it over his shoulder.

Soon Bill saw a gila monster.

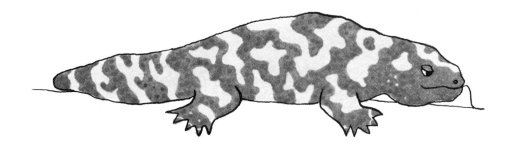

He twisted the snake into a loop.

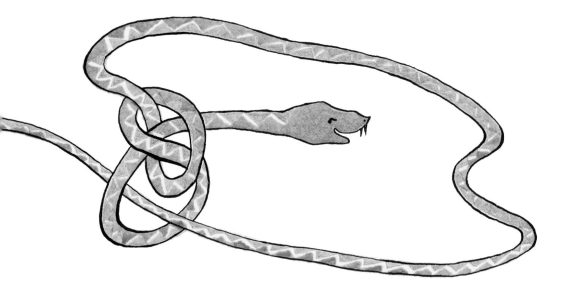

He twirled it around his head
and threw it.

The loop caught the monster.

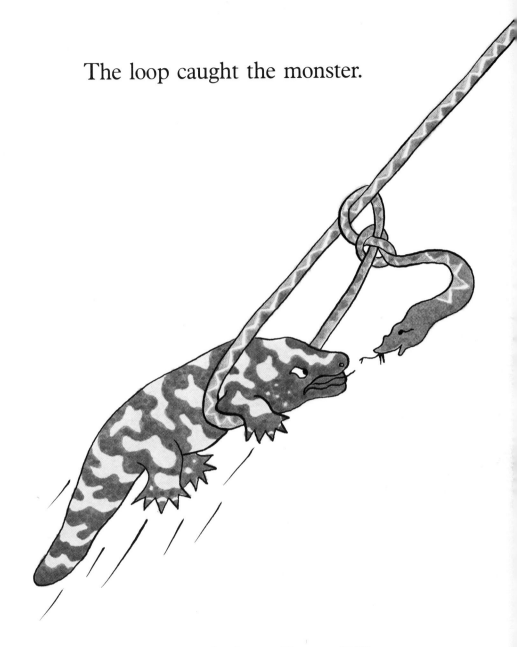

And that is how Pecos Bill
invented the lasso.

Bill and Curly Joe traveled on.
A mountain lion
jumped from a ledge
onto Bill's back.

Bill and the lion rolled on the ground.

They clawed one another.

Bill pulled out handfuls of lion fur

and threw them into the lion's eyes.

There was so much fur flying

that the sky grew dark.

"I give up," roared the lion.

"I just wanted to ride on your back."

"Well," replied Pecos Bill,
"I would rather ride on yours."
He jumped on the lion
and the lion bounded off.
Curly Joe was left behind.

In no time,

Bill, the snake, and the lion

came to the camp

of the Hell's Gulch gang.

The outlaws were scared.

Bill was hungry.

He ate all

the gang's beans.

He drank a gallon
of boiling coffee
out of the pot.
Then he wiped
his mouth
with a cactus.

"Who's boss here?" he asked.

"I was, but you is," Gun Smith said.

"Good," said Bill.

Just then Curly Joe came riding up.

"Meet Curly Joe," Bill said.

"Do you boys have any cattle?"
Curly Joe asked.

"Nope," said Bean Pole, the cook.

"Why don't we trap some stray ones?"
asked Gun Smith.

"How do you do that?"
said Pecos Bill.

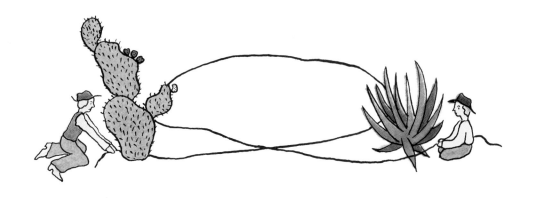

"We lay a chain on the ground
in a circle.
We hide and wait.

When a cow or bull
steps into the circle,

we pull the chain tight.

The animal trips and we jump it.

But sometimes it's a long wait

till one comes."

Pecos Bill knew a better way.

He rode off and lassoed

a dozen longhorn steers.

That's when he invented

cattle roping.

But the rattler was too short
to rope more than one steer at a time.
So Bill cut some cowhides into strips.
He tied the strips together
until he had a very long rope.

Now Bill could lasso anything.

He caught an eagle in flight.

He flicked the horns off toads.

He lassoed an entire herd
of wild cattle
in a single throw.

He brought so many cattle
to the ranch,
the men couldn't count them.

"Now that you are a proper cowboy,
you need a horse," Curly Joe said.
"Yep," Bill agreed.
"I heard of a mustang
that no one can catch.
Maybe you can get him,"
Curly Joe said.
Bill started off at once.
He could run
a hundred miles an hour.
He tracked that mustang from
Texas to Montana and back.

In Colorado, the mustang stopped
for a drink.
Bill said, "You're the fastest horse
that ever was
and I'm the greatest cowboy.
Let's team up."
And they did.

The Hell's Gulch gang
didn't like hard work.
There were too many cattle to watch.
Pecos Bill fixed that.
He lined up twenty prairie dogs.

As fast as a prairie dog dug a hole,

Bill filled it with a fence post.

That made the prairie dog mad.

It ran to the head of the

line and dug another hole.

Soon the fence went all around
Pinnacle Peak mountain.
Bill herded all the cattle
behind the fence.
They grazed around the mountain.
They couldn't wander away.
They couldn't get lost.
Sometimes a cow rolled
down a steep slope.
The cowboys put it
back on its feet.
That was the only work
they had to do.

A tornado tore through Oklahoma.
Bill heard it coming.
He climbed a pine tree and waited.
The tornado sucked the tree
up into its funnel.
There were wagons, cattle, trees,
houses, and even a steam engine
whirling around in it.
Bill crept up and out
onto the tornado's back.

"Yip-ee-i-ee what a ride!"

he shouted.

They crossed New Mexico,

Arizona, and California.

The storm blew down forests.

It knocked over mountains.

It flooded rivers.

But it couldn't throw Bill.

So it rained away.

Bill slid down a flash of lightning.

He landed with a thump.

The earth cracked.

And there was the Grand Canyon.

Bill saw Slue Foot Sue
riding a giant catfish
down the Rio Grande.
He was so impressed
that he asked her
to marry him.

On their wedding day

Sue wanted to ride Bill's mustang.

Bill was worried, but he gave in.

Sue was wearing her wedding dress.

Bustles were in fashion at the time.

Women wore wire frames

under their skirts

to make them stand out.

As soon as Sue got on the horse,

it bucked.

She fell off and landed on her bustle.

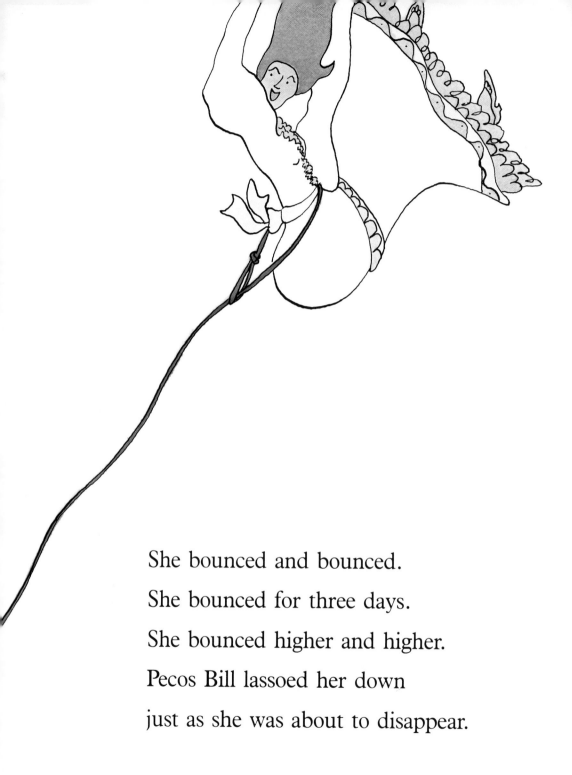

She bounced and bounced.

She bounced for three days.

She bounced higher and higher.

Pecos Bill lassoed her down

just as she was about to disappear.

Pecos Bill and Sue
started ranches all over the west.
Gun Smith was the foreman of one.
Curly Joe ran another.

They fenced off New Mexico
as a corral for newborn calves.
They used Arizona as a pasture.
The lion went back
to the Rocky Mountains.
But the rattlesnake still
traveled on Bill's shoulder
wherever he went.